IF FOUND, PLEASE RETURN THIS BOOK TO:

OR CONTACT VIA EMAIL:

UNION SQUARE & CO. and the distinctive Union Square & Co. logo
are trademarks of Sterling Publishing Co., Inc.

Union Square & Co., LLC, is a subsidiary of Sterling Publishing Co., Inc.

ISBN 978-1-4549-5374-6

For information about custom editions, special sales, and premium purchases, please contact specialsales@unionsquareandco.com.

Printed in India

2 4 6 8 10 9 7 5 3 1

unionsquareandco.com

Cover design and illustrations by Jim Tierney
Interior design by Christine Heun

Thy Own Life's Key

"I know nothing in the world that
has as much power as a word.
Sometimes I write one, and I look at it,
until it begins to shine."

—Emily Dickinson

Thy Own Life's Key

A FIVE-YEAR JOURNAL FOR BOOK LOVERS

UNION SQUARE & CO.
NEW YORK

JANUARY 1

"Hope smiles from the threshold of the new year to come."

—Alfred, Lord Tennyson, *The Foresters, or Robin Hood and Maid Marian*, 1892

20 __ __

20 __ __

20 __ __

20 __ __

20 __ __

JANUARY 2

"There is really no such thing as bad weather, only different kinds of good weather."

—John Rushkin, lecture at Oxford, 1883

20 __ __

20 __ __

20 __ __

20 __ __

20 __ __

JANUARY 3

"Love all, trust a few; / Do wrong to none: be able for thine enemy / Rather in power than use, and keep thy friend / Under thy own life's key."

—William Shakespeare, *All's Well That Ends Well*, 1623

20 __ __

20 __ __

20 __ __

20 __ __

20 __ __

JANUARY 4

"Forbid us something and that thing we desire."

—Geoffrey Chaucer, *The Canterbury Tales*, 1392

20 __ __

20 __ __

20 __ __

20 __ __

20 __ __

JANUARY 5

"Nature is full of genius, full of the divinity;
so that not a snowflake escapes its fashioning hand."

—Henry David Thoreau, journal entry, January 5, 1856

20 __ __

20 __ __

20 __ __

20 __ __

20 __ __

JANUARY 6

"Perchance he for whom this bell tolls may be so ill that he knows not it tolls for him."

—John Donne, *Devotions Upon Emergent Occasions*, 1623

20 __ __

20 __ __

20 __ __

20 __ __

20 __ __

JANUARY 7

"If Eve did err, it was for knowledge's sake."

—Aemilla Lanyer, *Eve's Apology in Defense of Women*, 1611

20 __ __

20 __ __

20 __ __

20 __ __

20 __ __

JANUARY 8

"We may brave human laws, but cannot resist natural ones."

—Jules Verne, *Twenty Thousand Leagues Under the Sea*, 1870

20 __ __

20 __ __

20 __ __

20 __ __

20 __ __

JANUARY 9

"Men who have a great deal of wit and prompt memories have not always the clearest judgment or deepest reason."

—John Locke, "An Essay Concerning Human Understanding," 1689

20 __ __

20 __ __

20 __ __

20 __ __

20 __ __

JANUARY 10

"That's a trail nothing but a nose can follow."

—James Fenimore Cooper, *The Last of the Mohicans*, 1826

20 __ __

20 __ __

20 __ __

20 __ __

20 __ __

JANUARY 11

"Be Homer's works your study and delight,
Read them by day, and meditate by night."

—Alexander Pope, "An Essay on Criticism," 1709

20 __ __

20 __ __

20 __ __

20 __ __

20 __ __

JANUARY 12

"Wherever he went he met gaiety and kindness, and heard the song of joy or the laugh of carelessness."

—Samuel Johnson, *Rasselas*, 1792

20__ __

20__ __

20__ __

20__ __

20__ __

JANUARY 13

"There is a stubbornness about me that never can bear to be frightened at the will of others. My courage always rises at every attempt to intimidate me."

—Jane Austen, *Pride and Prejudice*, 1813

20 __ __

20 __ __

20 __ __

20 __ __

20 __ __

JANUARY 14

"Can any man be courageous who has the fear of death in him?"

—Plato, *The Republic*, 375 BCE

20 __ __

20 __ __

20 __ __

20 __ __

20 __ __

JANUARY 15

"If we had no winter, the spring would not be so pleasant:
if we did not sometimes taste of adversity, prosperity would not be so welcome."

—Anne Bradstreet, *Meditations Divine and Moral*, 1867

20 __ __

20 __ __

20 __ __

20 __ __

20 __ __

JANUARY 16

"Patience will achieve more than force."

—Edmund Burke, "Reflections on the Revolution in France," 1790

20 __ __

20 __ __

20 __ __

20 __ __

20 __ __

JANUARY 17

"I have heard what the talkers were talking, the talk of the beginning and the end, / But I do not talk of the beginning or the end."

—Walt Whitman, *Song of Myself*, 1855

20 __ __

20 __ __

20 __ __

20 __ __

20 __ __

JANUARY 18

"We must come down from our heights, and leave our straight paths, for the byways and low places of life, if we would learn truths by strong contrasts."

—Richard Henry Dana Jr., *Two Years Before the Mast*, 1840

20 __ __

20 __ __

20 __ __

20 __ __

20 __ __

JANUARY 19

"Every single man, male and female,
is a perfect creature of himself."

—Gerrard Winstanley, *The True Levelers' Standard Advanced*, 1649

20 __ __

20 __ __

20 __ __

20 __ __

20 __ __

JANUARY 20

"With jest and compliment they conversed and cast off care; to the table soon they went; fresh dainties wait them there."

—Author unknown, *Sir Gawain and the Green Knight*, ca. 1375

20 __ __

20 __ __

20 __ __

20 __ __

20 __ __

JANUARY 21

"See now, how men lay blame upon us Gods
for what is after all nothing but their own folly."

—Homer, *The Odyssey*, ca. seventh century BCE

20 __ __

20 __ __

20 __ __

20 __ __

20 __ __

JANUARY 22

"I care for myself. The more solitary, the more friendless, the more unsustained I am, the more I will respect myself."

—Charlotte Brontë, *Jane Eyre*, 1847

20 __ __

20 __ __

20 __ __

20 __ __

20 __ __

JANUARY 23

"As I have always held it a crime to anticipate evils,
I will believe it a good comfortable road until I am compelled to believe differently."

—Merriweather Lewis, diary entry, 1805

20 __ __

20 __ __

20 __ __

20 __ __

20 __ __

JANUARY 24

"O wonder! How many goodly creatures are there here!
How beauteous mankind is!"

William Shakespeare, *The Tempest*, ca. 1610

20 __ __

20 __ __

20 __ __

20 __ __

20 __ __

JANUARY 25

"I have seen wicked men and fools, a great many of both; and I believe they both get paid in the end; but the fools first."

—Robert Louis Stevenson, *Kidnapped*, 1886

20 __ __

20 __ __

20 __ __

20 __ __

20 __ __

JANUARY 26

"A fool can ask more questions than the wisest can answer."

—Jonathan Swift, *Polite Conversation*, 1738

20 __ __

20 __ __

20 __ __

20 __ __

20 __ __

JANUARY 27

"I am neither condemning greatness, nor envying it, but gratefully and cheerfully enjoying what I am."

—Elizabeth Robinson Montagu, correspondence, 1770

20__ __

20__ __

20__ __

20__ __

20__ __

JANUARY 28

"Despotism increases in severity with the number of despots; the responsibility is more divided, and the claims are more numerous."

—William Wells Brown, *Clotel; or, The President's Daughter*, 1853

20 __ __

20 __ __

20 __ __

20 __ __

20 __ __

JANUARY 29

"In her voice, as in her eyes, there was that softness and gravity which is found in people continually concentrated on some cherished pursuit."

—Leo Tolstoy, *Anna Karenina*, 1878

20 __ __

20 __ __

20 __ __

20 __ __

20 __ __

JANUARY 30

"If there must be trouble, let it be in my day, that my child may have peace."

—Thomas Paine, *The American Crisis*, 1777

20 __ __

20 __ __

20 __ __

20 __ __

20 __ __

JANUARY 31

"When a man sees God in all beings and all beings in God, and also God dwelling in his own Soul, how can he hate any living thing?"

Author unknown, *The Upanishads*, ca. seventh century BCE

20 __ __

20 __ __

20 __ __

20 __ __

20 __ __

FEBRUARY 1

"And all we met was fair and good,
And all was good that Time could bring."

—Alfred, Lord Tennyson, *In Memoriam A.H.H.*, 1850

20 __ __

20 __ __

20 __ __

20 __ __

20 __ __

FEBRUARY 2

"Appear at points which the enemy must hasten to defend; march swiftly to places where you are not expected."

—Sun Tzu, *The Art of War*, sixth century BCE

20 __ __

20 __ __

20 __ __

20 __ __

20 __ __

FEBRUARY 3

"The bird that would soar above the level plain of tradition and prejudice must have strong wings."

—Kate Chopin, *The Awakening*, 1899

20__ __

20__ __

20__ __

20__ __

20__ __

FEBRUARY 4

"Nature sometimes mingles her effects and her spectacles with our actions with somber and intelligent appropriateness, as though she desired to make us reflect."

—Victor Hugo, *Les Misérables*, 1887

20 __ __

20 __ __

20 __ __

20 __ __

20 __ __

FEBRUARY 5

"But I could not hide / My quickening inner life from those at watch. / They saw a light at a window now and then, / They had not set there."

—Elizabeth Barrett Browning, *Aurora Leigh*, 1857

20 __ __

20 __ __

20 __ __

20 __ __

20 __ __

FEBRUARY 6

"No man for any considerable period can wear one face to himself, and another to the multitude, without finally getting bewildered as to which may be the true."

—Nathaniel Hawthorne, *The Scarlet Letter*, 1850

20 __ __

20 __ __

20 __ __

20 __ __

20 __ __

FEBRUARY 7

"I am the Cat who walks by himself, and all places are alike to me."

—Rudyard Kipling, "The Cat That Walked by Himself," 1902

20 __ __

20 __ __

20 __ __

20 __ __

20 __ __

FEBRUARY 8

"And, after all, what is a lie? 'Tis but / The truth in masquerade; and I defy / Historians, heroes, lawyers, priests, to put / A fact without some leaven of a lie."

—Lord Byron, *Don Juan*, 1819

20 __ __

20 __ __

20 __ __

20 __ __

20 __ __

FEBRUARY 9

"The whole interest of reason, speculative as well as practical, is centered in the three following questions: I. What can I know? 2. What ought I to do? 3. What may I hope?"

—Immanuel Kant, *Critique of Pure Reason*, 1781

20__ __

20__ __

20__ __

20__ __

20__ __

FEBRUARY 10

"And certainly, the mistakes that we male and female mortals make when we have our own way might fairly raise some wonder that we are so fond of it."

—George Eliot, *Middlemarch*, 1871

20 __ __

20 __ __

20 __ __

20 __ __

20 __ __

FEBRUARY 11

"But the phoenix fledgling shall fall to the earth /
And the sleeping dragon shall soar to the sky /
There shall be successes and failures / For such is the eternal law."

—Luo Guanzhong, *Romance of the Three Kingdoms*, ca. fourteenth century

20__ __

20__ __

20__ __

20__ __

20__ __

FEBRUARY 12

"Writing, the art of communicating thoughts to the mind through the eye, is the great invention of the world . . . enabling us to converse with the dead, the absent, and the unborn, at all distances of time and space."

—Abraham Lincoln, "Second Lecture on Discoveries and Inventions," 1860

20 __ __

20 __ __

20 __ __

20 __ __

20 __ __

FEBRUARY 13

"I never could have done what I have done, without
the habits of punctuality, order, and diligence,
without the determination to concentrate myself on one object at a time."

—Charles Dickens, *David Copperfield*, 1850

20 __ __

20 __ __

20 __ __

20 __ __

20 __ __

FEBRUARY 14

"If I loved you less, I might be able to talk about it more."

—Jane Austen, *Emma*, 1815

20 __ __

20 __ __

20 __ __

20 __ __

20 __ __

FEBRUARY 15

"Moralizing I observed then that 'all that glitters is not gold.' Mr. Ballou said I could go further than that and lay it up among my treasures of knowledge that nothing that glitters is gold."

—Mark Twain, *Roughing It*, 1872

20 __ __

20 __ __

20 __ __

20 __ __

20 __ __

FEBRUARY 16

"He has the merit—if it is one—of saying exactly what he means."

—E. M. Forster, *A Room with a View*, 1908

20 __ __

20 __ __

20 __ __

20 __ __

20 __ __

FEBRUARY 17

"Look to yourself, unless you are destined to be the sport of the winds."

—Horace, "Ode XIV," 23 BCE

20 __ __

20 __ __

20 __ __

20 __ __

20 __ __

FEBRUARY 18

"I have heard say that she whom commonly they call Fortune is a drunken whimsical jade, and, what is more, blind, and therefore neither sees what she does, nor knows whom she casts down or whom she sets up."

—Miguel de Cervantes, *Don Quixote*, 1612

20 __ __

20 __ __

20 __ __

20 __ __

20 __ __

FEBRUARY 19

"When one side only of a story is heard and often repeated, the human mind becomes impressed with it insensibly."

—George Washington, letter to Edmund Pendleton, 1795

20 __ __

20 __ __

20 __ __

20 __ __

20 __ __

FEBRUARY 20

"Sage follows on in the footsteps of sage; one hero just steps out of his triumphal car, to make way for the hero who comes after him."

—Washington Irving, *Knickerbocker's History of New York*, 1809

20 __ __

20 __ __

20 __ __

20 __ __

20 __ __

FEBRUARY 21

"Children have the strangest adventures without being troubled by them."

—J. M. Barrie, *Peter Pan*, 1911

20 __ __

20 __ __

20 __ __

20 __ __

20 __ __

FEBRUARY 22

"She had the power of silent sympathy. That sounds rather dull, I know, but it's not so dull as it sounds. It just means that a person is able to know that you are unhappy, and to love you extra on that account."

—E. Nesbit, *The Railway Children*, 1924

20 __ __

20 __ __

20 __ __

20 __ __

20 __ __

FEBRUARY 23

"She had a desire to leave the past behind her and, as she said to herself, to begin afresh. This desire indeed was not a birth of the present occasion; it was as familiar as the sound of the rain upon the window."

—Henry James, *The Portrait of a Lady*, 1881

20 __ __ ____________________

20 __ __ ____________________

20 __ __ ____________________

20 __ __ ____________________

20 __ __ ____________________

FEBRUARY 24

"He who sees, / How action may be rest, rest action—he / Is wisest amid his kind; he hath the truth!"

—Krishna-Dwaipayan Vyasa, *Mahabharata*, ca. third century BCE

20 __ __

20 __ __

20 __ __

20 __ __

20 __ __

FEBRUARY 25

"It is easy in the world to live after the world's opinion; it is easy in solitude to live after our own; but the great man is he who in the midst of the crowd keeps with perfect sweetness the independence of solitude."

—Ralph Waldo Emerson, "Self-Reliance," 1841

20 __ __

20 __ __

20 __ __

20 __ __

20 __ __

FEBRUARY 26

"No living creature is naturally greedy, except from fear of want—or in the case of human beings, from vanity."

—Sir Thomas More, *Utopia*, 1551

20__ __

20__ __

20__ __

20__ __

20__ __

FEBRUARY 27

"'What a fool you must be,' said my head to my heart, or my sterner to my softer self."

—Anne Brontë, *Agnes Grey*, 1847

20 __ __

20 __ __

20 __ __

20 __ __

20 __ __

FEBRUARY 28

"Think not, is my eleventh commandment; and sleep when you can, is my twelfth."

—Herman Melville, *Moby Dick*, 1851

20 __ __

20 __ __

20 __ __

20 __ __

20 __ __

FEBRUARY 29, LEAP YEAR

"If not now, when?"

Hillel the Elder, *Talmud*, ca. first century CE

20 __ __

MARCH 1

"If they mean that some Men are superior to some Women, this is no great discovery; had they turn'd the tables, they might have seen that some Women are superior to Some Men."

—Mary Astell, *Some Reflections upon Marriage*, 1700

20 __ __

20 __ __

20 __ __

20 __ __

20 __ __

MARCH 2

"If a man's character is to be abused, say what you will, there's nobody like a relative to do the business."

—William Makepeace Thackeray, *Vanity Fair*, 1848

20 __ __

20 __ __

20 __ __

20 __ __

20 __ __

MARCH 3

"The world is full of obvious things which nobody by any chance ever observes."

—Arthur Conan Doyle, *The Hound of the Baskervilles*, 1902

20 __ __

20 __ __

20 __ __

20 __ __

20 __ __

MARCH 4

"Being persuaded that the men of their time knew everything they would ever know . . . they confidently built their reveries upon the general opinions of their own country and their own age."

—Marquis de Condorcet, *Sketch for a Historical Picture of the Progress of the Human Mind*, 1794

20 __ __

20 __ __

20 __ __

20 __ __

20 __ __

MARCH 5

"Twice or thrice had I lov'd thee,
Before I knew thy face or name."

—John Donne, "Air and Angels," 1633

20 __ __

20 __ __

20 __ __

20 __ __

20 __ __

MARCH 6

"As pride sometimes is hid under humility,
Idleness is often covered by turbulence and hurry."

—Samuel Johnson, "On Idleness," 1750

20__ __

20__ __

20__ __

20__ __

20__ __

MARCH 7

"It sounds plausible enough tonight, but wait until tomorrow. Wait for the common sense of the morning."

—H. G. Wells, *The Time Machine*, 1895

20 __ __

20 __ __

20 __ __

20 __ __

20 __ __

MARCH 8

"What I like doing best is Nothing."

—A. A. Milne, *The House at Pooh Corner*, 1928

20 __ __

20 __ __

20 __ __

20 __ __

20 __ __

MARCH 9

"Canst thou with lying flattery rule me, / Until, self-pleased, myself I see, / Canst thou with rich enjoyment fool me, / Let that day be the last for me!"

—Johann Wolfgang von Goethe, *Faust*, 1808

20 __ __

20 __ __

20 __ __

20 __ __

20 __ __

MARCH 10

"Facts alone are wanted in life. Plant nothing else, and root out everything else."

—Charles Dickens, *Hard Times*, 1854

20 __ __

20 __ __

20 __ __

20 __ __

20 __ __

MARCH 11

"The lovers of the chase say that the hare feels more agony during the pursuit of the greyhounds, than when she is struggling in their fangs."

—Sir Walter Scott, *Ivanhoe*, 1819

20 __ __

20 __ __

20 __ __

20 __ __

20 __ __

MARCH 12

"The Empire of Love, said she, like the Empire of Honour is govern'd by Laws of its own, which have no Dependence upon, or Relation to any other."

—Charlotte Lennox, *The Female Quixote*, 1752

20 __ __

20 __ __

20 __ __

20 __ __

20 __ __

MARCH 13

"We are not going in circles, we are going upwards.
The path is a spiral; we have already climbed many steps."

—Herman Hesse, *Siddhartha*, 1922

20 __ __

20 __ __

20 __ __

20 __ __

20 __ __

MARCH 14

"Selfishness must always be forgiven, you know, because there is no hope of a cure."

—Jane Austen, *Mansfield Park*, 1814

20__ __

20__ __

20__ __

20__ __

20__ __

MARCH 15

"And since you know you cannot see yourself, / So well as by reflection, I, your glass, / Will modestly discover to yourself, / That of yourself which you yet know not of."

—William Shakespeare, *Julius Caesar*, 1623

20__ __

20__ __

20__ __

20__ __

20__ __

MARCH 16

"The tops of mountains are among the unfinished parts of the globe, whither it is a slight insult to the gods to climb and pry into their secrets, and try their effect on our humanity."

—Henry David Thoreau, *The Maine Woods*, 1864

20 __ __

20 __ __

20 __ __

20 __ __

20 __ __

MARCH 17

"I know for certain, that before I was humbled
I was like a stone lying in deep mire."

—St. Patrick, *The Confession of St. Patrick*, fourth century CE

20 __ __

20 __ __

20 __ __

20 __ __

20 __ __

MARCH 18

"Wisely and slow, they stumble that run fast."

—William Shakespeare, *Romeo and Juliet*, 1597

20 __ __

20 __ __

20 __ __

20 __ __

20 __ __

MARCH 19

"Speculations are profitless."

—Oscar Wilde, *The Importance of Being Earnest*, 1899

20 __ __

20 __ __

20 __ __

20 __ __

20 __ __

MARCH 20

"Believe nothing you hear, and only half that you see."

—Edgar Allan Poe, "The System of Doctor Tarr and Professor Fether," 1849

20__ __

20__ __

20__ __

20__ __

20__ __

MARCH 21

"Often, the less there is to justify a traditional custom, the harder it is to get rid of it."

—Mark Twain, *The Adventures of Tom Sawyer*, 1876

20 __ __

20 __ __

20 __ __

20 __ __

20 __ __

MARCH 22

"Life appears to me too short
to be spent in nursing animosity or registering wrongs."

—Charlotte Brontë, *Jane Eyre*, 1847

20 __ __ ______________________________

20 __ __ ______________________________

20 __ __ ______________________________

20 __ __ ______________________________

20 __ __ ______________________________

MARCH 23

"Nothing happened. I did not expect anything to happen.
I was something that lay under the sun and felt it . . . and I did not
want to be anything more. I was entirely happy."

—Willa Cather, *My Ántonia*, 1918

20__ __

20__ __

20__ __

20__ __

20__ __

MARCH 24

"In his blue gardens men and girls came and went
like moths among the whisperings and the champagne and the stars."

—F. Scott Fitzgerald, *The Great Gatsby*, 1925

20 __ __

20 __ __

20 __ __

20 __ __

20 __ __

MARCH 25

"The great secret, Eliza, is not having bad manners or good manners or any other particular sort of manners, but having the same manner for all human souls."

—George Bernard Shaw, *Pygmalion*, 1912

20 __ __

20 __ __

20 __ __

20 __ __

20 __ __

MARCH 26

"It is my belief no man ever understands quite his own artful dodges to escape from the grim shadow of self-knowledge."

—Joseph Conrad, *Lord Jim*, 1900

20 __ __

20 __ __

20 __ __

20 __ __

20 __ __

MARCH 27

"The spark that alights by chance on a powder keg does not produce so terrible an effect. The finger ready to light the fatal spark over you or me is perhaps raised."

—Denis Diderot, "This is Not a Story," 1772

20__ __

20__ __

20__ __

20__ __

20__ __

MARCH 28

"The mind commands the body and is instantly obeyed.
The mind commands itself and meets resistance."

—St. Augustine of Hippo, *Confessions*, ca. 400 CE

20 __ __

20 __ __

20 __ __

20 __ __

20 __ __

MARCH 29

"Freedom of choice is the essence of all accountability."

—Frederick Douglass, *My Bondage and My Freedom*, 1855

20 __ __

20 __ __

20 __ __

20 __ __

20 __ __

MARCH 30

"Will you your servant leave? Think but on this; / Who wears love's crown, must not do so amiss, / But seek their good, who on thy force do lie."

—Lady Mary Wroth, "Yet Is There Hope, Then Love But Play Thy Part," 1621

20 __ __

20 __ __

20 __ __

20 __ __

20 __ __

MARCH 31

"From any crime to its author there is a trail."

—Dashiell Hammett, "Bodies Piled Up," 1923

20 __ __

20 __ __

20 __ __

20 __ __

20 __ __

APRIL 1

"The sweet and bitter fool / Will presently appear; /
The one in motley here, / The other found out there."

—William Shakespeare, *King Lear*, 1608

20 __ __

20 __ __

20 __ __

20 __ __

20 __ __

APRIL 2

"Active valour may often be the present of nature;
but such patient diligence can be the fruit only of habit and discipline."

—Edward Gibbon, *The History of the Decline and Fall of the Roman Empire*, 1776

20 __ __

20 __ __

20 __ __

20 __ __

20 __ __

APRIL 3

"Thus strangely are our souls constructed,
and by such slight ligaments are we bound to prosperity or ruin."

—Mary Wollstonecraft Shelley, *Frankenstein*, 1818

20__ __

20__ __

20__ __

20__ __

20__ __

APRIL 4

"An adventure after my own heart, though so far the head and the tail of it are well hid, and the middle past all understanding!"

—Gertrude Barrows Bennett, *The Citadel of Fear*, 1918

20 __ __

20 __ __

20 __ __

20 __ __

20 __ __

APRIL 5

"For myth changes while custom remains constant; men continue to do what their fathers did before them, though the reasons on which their fathers acted have been long forgotten."

—Sir James George Frazer, *The Golden Bough*, 1890

20 __ __

20 __ __

20 __ __

20 __ __

20 __ __

APRIL 6

"It was not the thorn bending to the honeysuckles,
but the honeysuckles embracing the thorn."

—Emily Brontë, *Wuthering Heights*, 1847

20 __ __

20 __ __

20 __ __

20 __ __

20 __ __

APRIL 7

"She generally gave herself very good advice, (though she very seldom followed it)."

—Lewis Carroll, *Alice's Adventures in Wonderland*, 1865

20 __ __

20 __ __

20 __ __

20 __ __

20 __ __

APRIL 8

"I was not a hawk, although I might seem a hawk to those who had never hunted."

—Ernest Hemingway, "In Another Country," 1927

20 __ __

20 __ __

20 __ __

20 __ __

20 __ __

APRIL 9

"I do think that families
are the most beautiful things in all the world!"

—Louisa May Alcott, *Little Women*, 1868

20 __ __

20 __ __

20 __ __

20 __ __

20 __ __

APRIL 10

"It is a narrow mind which cannot look at a subject from various points of view."

—George Eliot, *Middlemarch*, 1871

20__ __

20__ __

20__ __

20__ __

20__ __

APRIL 11

"For it would seem—her case proved it—that we write, not with the fingers, but with the whole person. The nerve which controls the pen winds itself about every fibre of our being."

—Virginia Woolf, *Orlando*, 1928

20 __ __

20 __ __

20 __ __

20 __ __

20 __ __

APRIL 12

"For whatsoever from one place doth fall, / Is with the tide unto an other brought: / For there is nothing lost, that may be found, if sought."

—Edmund Spenser, *The Faerie Queene*, 1590

20 __ __

20 __ __

20 __ __

20 __ __

20 __ __

APRIL 13

"In peace, love tunes the shepherd's reed;
in war, he mounts the warrior's steed."

—Sir Walter Scott, *The Lay of the Last Minstrel*, 1805

20 __ __

20 __ __

20 __ __

20 __ __

20 __ __

APRIL 14

"Joy is the sweet voice; joy the luminous cloud; / We in ourselves rejoice!"

—Samuel Taylor Coleridge, "Dejection: An Ode," 1802

20 __ __

20 __ __

20 __ __

20 __ __

20 __ __

APRIL 15

"Every tax, however, is to the person who pays it a badge, not of slavery but of liberty. It denotes that he is a subject to government, indeed, but that, as he has some property, he cannot himself be the property of a master."

—Adam Smith, *The Wealth of Nations*, 1776

20 __ __

20 __ __

20 __ __

20 __ __

20 __ __

APRIL 16

"All by myself, wrapped in my thoughts, / And building castles in Spain and France."

—Charles d'Orléans, "Rondeaux," ca. 1440

20 __ __

20 __ __

20 __ __

20 __ __

20 __ __

APRIL 17

"Wisdom is oft-times nearer when we stoop; / Than when we soar."

—William Wordsworth, "The Excursion," 1814

20 __ __

20 __ __

20 __ __

20 __ __

20 __ __

APRIL 18

"I shall see you in three hours. Meanwhile, mio dolce amor, accept a thousand kisses, but give me none, for they fire my blood."

—Napoleon Bonaparte, letter to Josephine, 1796

20 __ __

20 __ __

20 __ __

20 __ __

20 __ __

APRIL 19

"Nothing is so beautiful as Spring; / When weeds, in wheels, shoot long and lovely and lush."

—Gerard Manley Hopkins, "Spring," 1892

20 __ __

20 __ __

20 __ __

20 __ __

20 __ __

APRIL 20

"Many things, having full reference, / To one consent, may work contrariously; / As many arrows, loosed several ways, / Come to one mark."

—William Shakespeare, *Henry V*, 1600

20 __ __

20 __ __

20 __ __

20 __ __

20 __ __

APRIL 21

"Follow a shadow, it still flies you; / Seem to fly it, it will pursue: / So court a mistress, she denies you; / Let her alone, she will court you."

—Ben Jonson, "The Shadow," sixteenth century

20 __ __

20 __ __

20 __ __

20 __ __

20 __ __

APRIL 22

"I am the master of my fate; I am the captain of my soul."

—William Ernest Henley, *Echoes of Life and Death*, 1908

20 __ __

20 __ __

20 __ __

20 __ __

20 __ __

APRIL 23

"Slivers of rain upon the pane; / Jade-green with sunlight, melt and flow; / Upward again:—they leave no stain; / Of storm or strain an hour ago."

—Hart Crane, "Pagan," 1917

20 __ __

20 __ __

20 __ __

20 __ __

20 __ __

APRIL 24

"Love truth, but pardon error."

—Voltaire, "Seven Discourses on Man," 1738

20 __ __

20 __ __

20 __ __

20 __ __

20 __ __

APRIL 25

"When Springtime came, red Robin built a nest,
And trilled a lover's song in sheer delight."

—Christina Rossetti, "A Wintry Sonnet," 1876

20 __ __

20 __ __

20 __ __

20 __ __

20 __ __

APRIL 26

"Here at our sea-washed, sunset gates shall stand / A mighty woman with a torch, whose flame / Is the imprisoned lightning, and her name, / Mother of Exiles."

—Emma Lazarus, "The New Colossus," 1903

20 __ __

20 __ __

20 __ __

20 __ __

20 __ __

APRIL 27

"Good wits jump; a word to the wise is enough."

—Miguel de Cervantes, *Don Quixote*, 1612

20 __ __

20 __ __

20 __ __

20 __ __

20 __ __

APRIL 28

"What passion can music not rise and quell?"

—John Dryden, "A Song for St. Cecilia's Day," 1687

20 __ __

20 __ __

20 __ __

20 __ __

20 __ __

APRIL 29

"Once the realization is accepted that even between the closest human beings infinite distances continue to exist, a wonderful living side by side can grow up."

—Rainer Maria Rilke, *Letters to a Young Poet*, 1929

20 __ __

20 __ __

20 __ __

20 __ __

20 __ __

APRIL 30

"When other helpers fail, and comforts flee,
Help of the helpless, oh, abide with me."

—Henry Francis Lyte, "Abide with Me," 1847

20 __ __

20 __ __

20 __ __

20 __ __

20 __ __

MAY 1

"Not kings and lords, but nations!
Not thrones and crowns, but men!"

—Ebenezer Elliott, "Corn Law Rhymes," 1831

20 __ __

20 __ __

20 __ __

20 __ __

20 __ __

MAY 2

"Therefore, like as May month flowereth and flourisheth in many gardens, so in like wise let every man of worship flourish his heart in this world."

—Sir Thomas Malory, *Le Morte D'Arthur*, 1485

20 __ __

20 __ __

20 __ __

20 __ __

20 __ __

MAY 3

"At every trifle, scorn to take offense."

—Alexander Pope, "An Essay on Criticism," 1711

20 __ __

20 __ __

20 __ __

20 __ __

20 __ __

MAY 4

"You must lie upon the daisies and discourse in novel phrases / of your complicated state of mind. / The meaning doesn't matter if it's only idle chatter / of a transcendental kind."

—W. S. Gilbert, *Patience; or, Bunthorne's Bride*, 1881

20 __ __

20 __ __

20 __ __

20 __ __

20 __ __

MAY 5

"Our forefathers had more leisure than we, and probably we have more than our descendants will have, who, for aught we know, may be able to put a 'girdle round about the earth in forty minutes.'"

—Madame Calderón de la Barca, *Life in Mexico*, 1843

20 __ __

20 __ __

20 __ __

20 __ __

20 __ __

MAY 6

"Thus weave for us a garment of brightness,
That we may walk fittingly where birds sing,
That we may walk fittingly where grass is green."

—Author unknown, "Song of the Sky Loom," Native American invocation, undated

20 __ __

20 __ __

20 __ __

20 __ __

20 __ __

MAY 7

"A wonderful fact to reflect upon, that every human creature is constituted to be that profound secret and mystery to every other."

—Charles Dickens, *A Tale of Two Cities*, 1859

20 __ __

20 __ __

20 __ __

20 __ __

20 __ __

MAY 8

"May I ask whether these pleasing attentions proceed from the impulse of the moment, or are the result of previous study?"

—Jane Austen, *Pride and Prejudice*, 1813

20 __ __

20 __ __

20 __ __

20 __ __

20 __ __

MAY 9

"I don't like work—no man does—but I like what is in work—the chance to find yourself."

—Joseph Conrad, *Heart of Darkness*, 1899

20 __ __

20 __ __

20 __ __

20 __ __

20 __ __

MAY 10

"Peace is more important than all justice; and peace was not made for the sake of justice, but justice for the sake of peace."

—Martin Luther, "On Marriage," 1530

20 __ __

20 __ __

20 __ __

20 __ __

20 __ __

MAY 11

"I believe in the forest, and in the meadow, and in the night in which the corn grows."

—Henry David Thoreau, "Walking," 1851

20 __ __

20 __ __

20 __ __

20 __ __

20 __ __

MAY 12

"Let the most absent-minded of men be plunged in his deepest reveries—stand that man upon his legs, set his feet a-going, and he will invariably lead you to water."

—Herman Melville, *Moby Dick*, 1851

20 __ __

20 __ __

20 __ __

20 __ __

20 __ __

MAY 13

"It would be an endless task to trace the variety of meannesses, cares, and sorrows into which women are plunged by the prevailing opinion that they were created rather to feel than reason."

—Mary Wollstonecraft, *A Vindication of the Rights of Woman*, 1792

20 __ __

20 __ __

20 __ __

20 __ __

20 __ __

MAY 14

"I never saw a wild thing sorry for itself. A small bird will drop frozen dead from a bough without ever having felt sorry for itself."

—D. H. Lawrence, "Self-Pity," 1909

20__ __

20__ __

20__ __

20__ __

20__ __

MAY 15

"I do like a little bit of butter on my bread!"

—A. A. Milne, *When We Were Very Young*, 1924

20 __ __

20 __ __

20 __ __

20 __ __

20 __ __

MAY 16

"Every man's condition is a solution in hieroglyphic to those inquiries he would put. He acts it as life, before he apprehends it as truth."

—Ralph Waldo Emerson, "Nature," 1849

20 __ __

20 __ __

20 __ __

20 __ __

20 __ __

MAY 17

"Burn from my brain and from my breast;
Sloth, and the cowardice that clings."

—G. K. Chesterton, "A Ballade of a Book-Reviewer," 1915

20 __ __

20 __ __

20 __ __

20 __ __

20 __ __

MAY 18

"Fly, Grecians, fly, your sails and oars employ,
And dream no more of heaven-defended Troy."

—Homer, *The Iliad*, eighth century BCE

20 __ __

20 __ __

20 __ __

20 __ __

20 __ __

MAY 19

"Behave in life as you would at a banquet. As something is being passed around it comes to you: stretch out your hand, take a portion politely."

—Epictetus, *The Enchiridion*, second century CE

20 __ __

20 __ __

20 __ __

20 __ __

20 __ __

MAY 20

"Most people live, whether physically, intellectually or morally, in a very restricted circle of their potential being."

—William James, *The Energies of Men*, 1907

20 __ __

20 __ __

20 __ __

20 __ __

20 __ __

MAY 21

"As for life, it is a battle and a sojourning in a strange land."

—Marcus Aurelius, *Meditations*, 167 CE

20 __ __

20 __ __

20 __ __

20 __ __

20 __ __

MAY 22

"The Greatest Happiness Principle holds that actions are right in proportion
as they tend to promote happiness,
wrong as they tend to produce the reverse of happiness."

—John Stuart Mill, "Utilitarianism," 1863

20 __ __

20 __ __

20 __ __

20 __ __

20 __ __

MAY 23

"It's fare thee well to old mother and fare thee well to father too;
I'm going for to ramble this wide world all through."

—Author unknown, "Pretty Saro," English (later Appalachian) folk ballad, seventeenth century CE

20 __ __

20 __ __

20 __ __

20 __ __

20 __ __

MAY 24

"Remember the Ladies, and be more generous and favorable to them than your ancestors. Do not put such unlimited power into the hands of the Husbands. Remember all Men would be tyrants if they could."

—Abigail Adams, letter to husband John Adams, 1776

20 __ __

20 __ __

20 __ __

20 __ __

20 __ __

MAY 25

"If man does indeed find within him a page written out, his first thoughts should be whether it is in a language he can read."

—Charles Mayo Ellis, "An Essay on Transcendentalism," 1842

20 __ __

20 __ __

20 __ __

20 __ __

20 __ __

MAY 26

"Accursed be he that first invented war."

—Christopher Marlowe, *Tamburlaine the Great*, 1590

20__ __

20__ __

20__ __

20__ __

20__ __

MAY 27

"The Poetry is in the pity. All a poet can do today is warn."

—Wilfred Owen, "The Poetry is in the pity . . . ," 1918

20 __ __

20 __ __

20 __ __

20 __ __

20 __ __

MAY 28

"It is not only fine feathers that make fine birds."

—Aesop, *Aesop's Fables*, sixth century BCE

20 __ __

20 __ __

20 __ __

20 __ __

20 __ __

MAY 29

"Nature contains the elements, in colour and form, of all pictures, as the keyboard contains the notes of all music."

—James McNeill Whistler, "Ten O'Clock," 1885

20 __ __

20 __ __

20 __ __

20 __ __

20 __ __

MAY 30

"They were going to look at war, the red animal—war. The blood-swollen god."

—Stephen Crane, *The Red Badge of Courage*, 1895

20 __ __

20 __ __

20 __ __

20 __ __

20 __ __

MAY 31

"Some there be that shadows kiss; / Such have but a shadow's bliss."

—William Shakespeare, *The Merchant of Venice*, 1596–97

20 __ __

20 __ __

20 __ __

20 __ __

20 __ __

JUNE 1

"Power has only one duty—to secure the social welfare of the people."

—Benjamin Disraeli, *Sybil, or the Two Nations*, 1845

20 __ __

20 __ __

20 __ __

20 __ __

20 __ __

JUNE 2

"I had never handled a tool in my life; and yet, in time, by labour, application, and contrivance, I found at last that I wanted nothing but I could have made it, especially if I had had tools."

—Daniel Defoe, *Robinson Crusoe*, 1719

20 __ __

20 __ __

20 __ __

20 __ __

20 __ __

JUNE 3

"Out of the Spawn of this Fish the best Caviare is made in Muscovy; tho' they also make it of the Spawn of the Sturgeons and Pikes."

—Adam Brand, *A Journal of the Embassy from Their Majesties John and Peter Alexievitz*, 1698

20 __ __

20 __ __

20 __ __

20 __ __

20 __ __

JUNE 4

"In countries where there is any popular Idea of Liberty, the universities are considered its stronghold, from their being the places where the young, active, hopeful, and aspiring meet."

—Harriet Martineau, *How to Observe Morals and Manners*, 1838

20 __ __

20 __ __

20 __ __

20 __ __

20 __ __

JUNE 5

"I believe that this life is not all; neither the beginning nor the end. I believe while I tremble; I trust while I weep."

—Charlotte Brontë, *Villette*, 1853

20 __ __

20 __ __

20 __ __

20 __ __

20 __ __

JUNE 6

"A man who keeps company with glaciers comes to feel tolerably insignificant by and by."

—Mark Twain, *A Tramp Abroad*, 1880

20 __ __

20 __ __

20 __ __

20 __ __

20 __ __

JUNE 7

"Remember that the best and greatest among mankind are those who do themselves no worldly good."

—Thomas Hardy, *Jude the Obscure*, 1894

20 __ __

20 __ __

20 __ __

20 __ __

20 __ __

JUNE 8

"On either side the river lie / Long fields of barley and of rye, / That clothe the wold and meet the sky."

—Alfred, Lord Tennyson, "The Lady of Shalott," 1832

20 __ __

20 __ __

20 __ __

20 __ __

20 __ __

JUNE 9

"There are only two or three human stories, and they go on repeating themselves as fiercely as if they had never happened before."

—Willa Cather, *O Pioneers!*, 1913

20 __ __

20 __ __

20 __ __

20 __ __

20 __ __

JUNE 10

"Faith without works is worse than nothing, / And as dead as a doornail unless the deed goes with it."

—William Langland, "Piers Plowman," ca. 1377

20 __ __

20 __ __

20 __ __

20 __ __

20 __ __

JUNE 11

"He prayeth well who loveth well; both man and bird and beast."

—Samuel Taylor Coleridge, *The Rime of the Ancient Mariner*, 1798

20__ __

20__ __

20__ __

20__ __

20__ __

JUNE 12

"I'll tell you how the sun rose / A Ribbon at a time."

—Emily Dickinson, poem no. 318, 1890

20 __ __

20 __ __

20 __ __

20 __ __

20 __ __

JUNE 13

"She walks in beauty, like the night / Of cloudless climes and starry skies."

—Lord Byron, "She Walks in Beauty," 1814

20 __ __

20 __ __

20 __ __

20 __ __

20 __ __

JUNE 14

"All shall be well, and all shall be well,
and all manner of thing shall be well."

—Julian of Norwich, *Revelations of Divine Love*, ca. 1393

20 __ __

20 __ __

20 __ __

20 __ __

20 __ __

JUNE 15

"I, too, sing America. / I am the darker brother. / They send me to eat in the kitchen / When company comes, / But I laugh, / And eat well, / And grow strong."

—Langston Hughes, "I, Too," 1926

20 __ __

20 __ __

20 __ __

20 __ __

20 __ __

JUNE 16

"I'll make it my business to write a letter one of those days to his mother or his aunt or whatever she is that will open her eye as wide as a gate. I'll tickle his catastrophe, believe you me."

—James Joyce, *Ulysses*, 1922

20 __ __

20 __ __

20 __ __

20 __ __

20 __ __

JUNE 17

"It is sometimes fortunate, that the means which are taken to produce certain effects upon the mind have a tendency directly opposite to what is expected."

—Maria Edgeworth, *Belinda*, 1801

20 __ __

20 __ __

20 __ __

20 __ __

20 __ __

JUNE 18

"Once, Zhuang Zhou dreamed he was a butterfly, a butterfly flitting and fluttering about, happy with himself and doing as he pleased. He didn't know that he was Zhuang Zhou."

—Zhuang Zhou, *Zhuangzi*, third century BCE

20 __ __

20 __ __

20 __ __

20 __ __

20 __ __

JUNE 19

"'And take you my head,' said he, 'and bear it even unto the White Mount, in London, and bury it there, with the face towards France.'"

—Author unknown, *Mabinogion*, Welsh folktales, ca. twelfth century CE

20 __ __

20 __ __

20 __ __

20 __ __

20 __ __

JUNE 20

"Anything one man can imagine, other men can make real."

—Jules Verne, *Around the World in Eighty Days*, 1873

20 __ __

20 __ __

20 __ __

20 __ __

20 __ __

JUNE 21

"For the strength of the Pack is the Wolf, and the strength of the Wolf is the Pack."

—Rudyard Kipling, *The Jungle Book*, 1894

20 __ __

20 __ __

20 __ __

20 __ __

20 __ __

JUNE 22

"He who had been alone in the sad, silent watches of the night was not now and never must be again alone."

—Zane Grey, *Riders of the Purple Sage*, 1912

20 __ __

20 __ __

20 __ __

20 __ __

20 __ __

JUNE 23

"They hail you as their morning star / Because you are the way you are. / If you return the sentiment, / They'll try to make you different."

—Dorothy Parker, "Men," 1926

20 __ __

20 __ __

20 __ __

20 __ __

20 __ __

JUNE 24

"With affection beaming in one eye, and calculation shining out of the other."

—Charles Dickens, *The Life and Adventures of Martin Chuzzlewit*, 1844

20 __ __

20 __ __

20 __ __

20 __ __

20 __ __

JUNE 25

"Life, within doors, has few pleasanter prospects than a neatly-arranged and well-provisioned breakfast-table."

—Nathaniel Hawthorne, *The House of the Seven Gables*, 1851

20 __ __

20 __ __

20 __ __

20 __ __

20 __ __

JUNE 26

"Twas difficult to find a rat;
With nature's debt unpaid."

—Jean de La Fontaine, *Fables*, 1668

20 __ __

20 __ __

20 __ __

20 __ __

20 __ __

JUNE 27

"If the name of wife appears more sacred and more valid, sweeter to me is ever the word friend."

—Heloise d'Argenteuil, *The Letters of Abelard and Heloise*, ca. twelfth century CE

20 __ __

20 __ __

20 __ __

20 __ __

20 __ __

JUNE 28

"Nothing can dwindle to nothing, as Nature restores one thing from the stuff of another."

—Lucretius, *On the Nature of Things*, first century BCE

20 __ __

20 __ __

20 __ __

20 __ __

20 __ __

JUNE 29

"Besides, nowadays, almost all capable people are terribly afraid of being ridiculous, and are miserable because of it."

—Fyodor Dostoyevsky, *The Brothers Karamazov*, 1879

20 __ __

20 __ __

20 __ __

20 __ __

20 __ __

JUNE 30

"What pleasure I from such obedience paid, / When Will and Reason (Reason also is choice) / Useless and vain, of freedom both despoild, / Made passive both, had servd necessitie / Not me."

—John Milton, *Paradise Lost*, 1667

20 __ __

20 __ __

20 __ __

20 __ __

20 __ __

JULY 1

"It is certainly not the least charm of a theory that it is refutable."

—Friedrich Nietzsche, *Beyond Good and Evil*, 1886

20 __ __

20 __ __

20 __ __

20 __ __

20 __ __

JULY 2

"Sudden glory is the passion which maketh those grimaces called laughter."

—Thomas Hobbes, *Leviathan*, 1651

20 __ __

20 __ __

20 __ __

20 __ __

20 __ __

JULY 3

"What good shall I do this day?"

—Benjamin Franklin, *Autobiography of Benjamin Franklin*, 1791

20 __ __

20 __ __

20 __ __

20 __ __

20 __ __

JULY 4

"I hold it that a little rebellion now and then is a good thing, and as necessary in the political world as storms in the physical."

—Thomas Jefferson, letter to James Madison, 1787

20__ __

20__ __

20__ __

20__ __

20__ __

JULY 5

"The summer hath his joys, and winter his delights; / Though love and all his pleasures are but toys, / They shorten tedious nights."

—Thomas Campion, *The Third and Fourth Booke of Ayres*, 1617

20 __ __

20 __ __

20 __ __

20 __ __

20 __ __

JULY 6

"Why do your tongues falter in maintenance of the right?"

—Harriet Jacobs, *Incidents in the Life of a Slave Girl*, 1861

20 __ __

20 __ __

20 __ __

20 __ __

20 __ __

JULY 7

"It was roses, roses, all the way."

—Robert Browning, "The Patriot," 1855

20 __ __

20 __ __

20 __ __

20 __ __

20 __ __

JULY 8

"Sweet are the thoughts that savour of content;
The quiet mind is richer than a crown."

—Robert Greene, "Farewell to Folly," 1591

20 __ __

20 __ __

20 __ __

20 __ __

20 __ __

JULY 9

"Of purple, red or yellow flower appears, / Unknown to thy soft bowers; / The odors of thy thousand flowers, / The wind's delight afford."

—Andrés Bello, "Ode to Tropical Agriculture," 1826

20 __ __

20 __ __

20 __ __

20 __ __

20 __ __

JULY 10

"Let other pens dwell on guilt and misery."

—Jane Austen, *Mansfield Park*, 1814

20 __ __

20 __ __

20 __ __

20 __ __

20 __ __

JULY 11

"If you look the right way, you can see that the whole world is a garden."

—Frances Hodgson Burnett, *The Secret Garden*, 1911

20 __ __ ____________________

20 __ __ ____________________

20 __ __ ____________________

20 __ __ ____________________

20 __ __ ____________________

JULY 12

"In appearance, at least, he being on all occasions glad to be at friendship with me, though we hate one another and know it on both sides."

—Samuel Pepys, *The Diary of Samuel Pepys*, 1660–69

20 __ __

20 __ __

20 __ __

20 __ __

20 __ __

JULY 13

"It is the nature of extreme self-lovers, as they will set a house on fire, and it were but to roast their eggs."

—Francis Bacon, "Of Wisdom for a Man's Self," 1625

20 __ __

20 __ __

20 __ __

20 __ __

20 __ __

JULY 14

"The two opposing kinds of pride confronting one another, I can see, even in this Bastille; the gentleman's, all negligent indifference; the peasant's, all trodden-down sentiment, and passionate revenge."

—Charles Dickens, *A Tale of Two Cities*, 1859

20 __ __

20 __ __

20 __ __

20 __ __

20 __ __

JULY 15

"Some people without brains do an awful lot of talking, don't you think?"

—L. Frank Baum, *The Wonderful Wizard of Oz*, 1900

20 __ __

20 __ __

20 __ __

20 __ __

20 __ __

JULY 16

"Kindred spirits are not so scarce as I used to think. It's splendid to find out there are so many of them in the world."

—L. M. Montgomery, *Anne of Green Gables*, 1908

20__ __

20__ __

20__ __

20__ __

20__ __

JULY 17

"'Getting up early all the time,' he thought, 'it makes you stupid. You've got to get enough sleep.'"

—Franz Kafka, *The Metamorphosis*, 1915

20 __ __

20 __ __

20 __ __

20 __ __

20 __ __

JULY 18

"After all, the best part of a holiday is perhaps not so much to be resting yourself, as to see all the other fellows busy working."

—Kenneth Grahame, *The Wind in the Willows*, 1908

20 __ __

20 __ __

20 __ __

20 __ __

20 __ __

JULY 19

"The books—the generous friends who met me without suspicion—the merciful masters who never used me ill!"

—Wilkie Collins, *Armadale*, 1866

20 __ __

20 __ __

20 __ __

20 __ __

20 __ __

JULY 20

"He is himself his own World, his own Universe; of any other than himself he can form no conception; he knows not Length, nor Breadth, nor Height."

—Edwin A. Abbott, *Flatland*, 1884

20 __ __

20 __ __

20 __ __

20 __ __

20 __ __

JULY 21

"I cannot well repeat how there I entered, / So full was I of slumber at the moment, / In which I had abandoned the true way."

—Dante, *The Divine Comedy*, 1319

20 __ __

20 __ __

20 __ __

20 __ __

20 __ __

JULY 22

"They seek him here, they seek him there, / Those Frenchies seek him everywhere. / Is he in heaven or is he in hell? / That damned elusive Pimpernel!"

—Baroness Orczy, *The Scarlet Pimpernel*, 1905

20 __ __

20 __ __

20 __ __

20 __ __

20 __ __

JULY 23

"But the future must be met, however stern and iron it be."

—Elizabeth Gaskell, *North and South*, 1855

20 __ __

20 __ __

20 __ __

20 __ __

20 __ __

JULY 24

"But I am I, and I won't subordinate my taste to the unanimous judgment of mankind. If I don't like a thing, I don't like it, that's all."

—Jack London, *Martin Eden*, 1909

20 __ __

20 __ __

20 __ __

20 __ __

20 __ __

JULY 25

"'Is that all?' said the fox. 'I am master of a hundred arts, and have into the bargain a sackful of cunning.'"

—The Brothers Grimm, "The Fox and the Cat," 1812

20 __ __

20 __ __

20 __ __

20 __ __

20 __ __

JULY 26

"In one respect at least the Martians are a happy people, they have no lawyers."

—Edgar Rice Burroughs, *A Princess of Mars*, 1912

20 __ __

20 __ __

20 __ __

20 __ __

20 __ __

JULY 27

"A sentence should contain no unnecessary words, a paragraph no unnecessary sentences, for the same reason that a drawing should have no unnecessary lines and a machine no unnecessary parts."

—William Strunk Jr. and E. B. White, *The Elements of Style*, 1918

20 __ __

20 __ __

20 __ __

20 __ __

20 __ __

JULY 28

"Our bodies are our gardens, to the which our wills are gardeners."

—William Shakespeare, *Othello*, 1622

20 __ __

20 __ __

20 __ __

20 __ __

20 __ __

JULY 29

"Good drinke is a medicine for all diseases."

—Thomas Nashe, *The Unfortunate Traveler*, 1594

20 __ __

20 __ __

20 __ __

20 __ __

20 __ __

JULY 30

"But time lessens all extremes, and reduces them to mediums and unconcern."

—Aphra Behn, *Oroonoko*, 1688

20 __ __

20 __ __

20 __ __

20 __ __

20 __ __

JULY 31

"Tyranny is the exercise of power beyond right, which no body can have a right to . . . not for the good of those who are under it, but for his own private separate advantage."

—John Locke, *Two Treatises of Government*, 1689

20 __ __

20 __ __

20 __ __

20 __ __

20 __ __

AUGUST 1

"Never neglect to keep the anniversaries of your ancestors, and make it your duty to provide for your children's future. Thus will you live to a good old age and be happy."

—Yei Theodora Ozaki, Japanese folktale, 1908

20 __ __

20 __ __

20 __ __

20 __ __

20 __ __

AUGUST 2

"I broke the spell that held me long, / The dear, dear witchery of song."

—William Cullen Bryant, "I Broke the Spell That Held Me Long," 1832

20 __ __

20 __ __

20 __ __

20 __ __

20 __ __

AUGUST 3

"When war assaults him serve him as liegemen:
By praise-worthy actions must honor be got."

—Author unknown, *Beowulf*, Old English epic poem, ca. tenth century CE

20 __ __

20 __ __

20 __ __

20 __ __

20 __ __

AUGUST 4

"Morning always promises miracles."

—Sinclair Lewis, *Elmer Gantry*, 1927

20 __ __

20 __ __

20 __ __

20 __ __

20 __ __

AUGUST 5

"A bystander often sees more of the game than those that play."

—Horace Walpole, *The Castle of Otranto*, 1764

20 __ __

20 __ __

20 __ __

20 __ __

20 __ __

AUGUST 6

"Hope in gates, hope in spoons, hope in doors, hope in tables, no hope in daintiness and determination. Hope in dates."

—Gertrude Stein, *Tender Buttons*, 1914

20 __ __

20 __ __

20 __ __

20 __ __

20 __ __

AUGUST 7

"For I hope my Friends will pardon me, when I declare, I know none of them without a Fault; and I should be sorry if I could imagine, I had any Friend who could not see mine."

—Henry Fielding, *Tom Jones*, 1749

20 __ __

20 __ __

20 __ __

20 __ __

20 __ __

AUGUST 8

"'Is there any chance of a drink itself?' asked Mr O'Connor."

—James Joyce, *Dubliners*, 1914

20 __ __

20 __ __

20 __ __

20 __ __

20 __ __

AUGUST 9

"The sentence past is most irrevocable,
A common thing, yet oh inevitable."

—Anne Bradstreet, "Before the Birth of One of Her Children," 1650

20 __ __

20 __ __

20 __ __

20 __ __

20 __ __

AUGUST 10

"I have the defect of being more sincere than persons wish."

—Molière, *The Misanthrope*, 1666

20 __ __

20 __ __

20 __ __

20 __ __

20 __ __

AUGUST 11

"I am large, I contain multitudes."

—Walt Whitman, *Leaves of Grass*, 1855

20 __ __

20 __ __

20 __ __

20 __ __

20 __ __

AUGUST 12

"It is just as if a curtain were suddenly raised and a drama began; or just as if I were suddenly transferred to another man's body and life, remembering past years of that life, and not cognizant of any other existence."

—Robert E. Howard, "The Dream Snake," 1928

20 __ __

20 __ __

20 __ __

20 __ __

20 __ __

AUGUST 13

"Surprises are foolish things. The pleasure is not enhanced, and the inconvenience is often considerable."

—Jane Austen, *Emma*, 1815

20 __ __

20 __ __

20 __ __

20 __ __

20 __ __

AUGUST 14

"Oh, be humble, my brother, in your prosperity!
Be gentle with those who are less lucky, if not more deserving."

—William Makepeace Thackeray, *Vanity Fair*, 1848

20 __ __

20 __ __

20 __ __

20 __ __

20 __ __

AUGUST 15

"Lay the proud usurpers low!
Tyrants fall in every foe!
Liberty's in every blow!"

—Robert Burns, "Scots Wha Hae," 1793

20 __ __

20 __ __

20 __ __

20 __ __

20 __ __

AUGUST 16

"Who has not cursed postmasters? Who has not demanded from them the fatal book in order to record in it unavailing complaints of their extortions, rudeness and unpunctuality?"

—Alexander Pushkin, *The Postmaster*, 1916

20 __ __

20 __ __

20 __ __

20 __ __

20 __ __

AUGUST 17

"True adventurers have never been plentiful. They who are set down in print as such have been mostly businessmen with newly invented methods."

—O. Henry, "The Green Door," 1906

20 __ __

20 __ __

20 __ __

20 __ __

20 __ __

AUGUST 18

"In the presence of a good man, think all the time how you might equal him. In the presence of a bad man, turn your gaze within!"

—Confucius, *The Analects*, ca. 479 BCE

20 __ __

20 __ __

20 __ __

20 __ __

20 __ __

AUGUST 19

"Fade far away, dissolve and quite forget / What thou among the leaves hast never known, / The weariness, the fever, and the fret."

—John Keats, "Ode to a Nightingale," 1819

20 __ __

20 __ __

20 __ __

20 __ __

20 __ __

AUGUST 20

"Three of the greatest failings, want of sense, of courage, or of vigilance."

—Thucydides, *History of the Peloponnesian War*, ca. 500 BCE

20 __ __

20 __ __

20 __ __

20 __ __

20 __ __

AUGUST 21

"She had no tolerance for scenes
which were not of her own making."

—Edith Wharton, *The House of Mirth*, 1905

20 __ __

20 __ __

20 __ __

20 __ __

20 __ __

AUGUST 22

"Only connect the prose and the passion, and both will be exalted, and human love will be seen at its highest. Live in fragments no longer."

—E. M. Forster, *Howards End*, 1910

20 __ __

20 __ __

20 __ __

20 __ __

20 __ __

AUGUST 23

"Yet this barbarous age contained in it
the germs of all that had been accomplished afterwards."

—Catherine Helen Spence, *A Week in the Future*, 1888

20 __ __

20 __ __

20 __ __

20 __ __

20 __ __

AUGUST 24

"Does dullness veil thee? Here a stone chamber invites thee into the world of dreams through an unseen door."

—Yoné Noguchi, *Voice of the Valley*, 1897

20 __ __

20 __ __

20 __ __

20 __ __

20 __ __

AUGUST 25

"Yet each man kills the thing he loves, / By each let this be heard, / Some do it with a bitter look, / Some with a flattering word."

—Oscar Wilde, "The Ballad of Reading Gaol," 1898

20 __ __

20 __ __

20 __ __

20 __ __

20 __ __

AUGUST 26

"Who is better able to know God than I myself, since He resides in my heart and is the very essence of my being? Such should be the attitude of one who is seeking."

—Author unknown, *The Upanishads*, ca. seventh century BCE

20 __ __

20 __ __

20 __ __

20 __ __

20 __ __

AUGUST 27

"Haven't you ever happened to come across in a book some vague notion that you've had, some obscure idea that returns from afar and that seems to express completely your most subtle feelings?"

—Gustave Flaubert, *Madame Bovary*, 1856

20 __ __

20 __ __

20 __ __

20 __ __

20 __ __

AUGUST 28

"I see in your existence the clearest, most express, and best-preserved form of the extraordinary in the world."

—Thomas Mann, *Royal Highness*, 1909

20__ __

20__ __

20__ __

20__ __

20__ __

AUGUST 29

"I am no bird; and no net ensnares me: I am a free human being with an independent will."

—Charlotte Brontë, *Jane Eyre*, 1847

20__ __

20__ __

20__ __

20__ __

20__ __

AUGUST 30

"I'll sing about those who are gay, and those who are sorrowful. My songs will tell you of all the good and evil that you do not see."

—Hans Christian Andersen, "The Nightingale," 1843

20 __ __

20 __ __

20 __ __

20 __ __

20 __ __

AUGUST 31

"Traveling—it leaves you speechless, then turns you into a storyteller."

—Ibn Battuta, *Rihlah (Travels)*, 1355

20 __ __

20 __ __

20 __ __

20 __ __

20 __ __

SEPTEMBER 1

"Up from the meadows rich with corn, / Clear in the cool September morn."

—John Greenleaf Whittier, "Barbara Frietchie," 1863

20__ __

20__ __

20__ __

20__ __

20__ __

SEPTEMBER 2

"Man is neither angel nor beast; and the misfortune is that he who would act the angel acts the beast."

—Blaise Pascal, *Thoughts*, 1669

20 __ __

20 __ __

20 __ __

20 __ __

20 __ __

SEPTEMBER 3

"All falsehood is a mask; and however well made the mask may be, with a little attention we may always succeed in distinguishing it from the true face."

—Alexandre Dumas, *The Three Musketeers*, 1844

20 __ __

20 __ __

20 __ __

20 __ __

20 __ __

SEPTEMBER 4

"The man that hath no music in himself, / Nor is not moved with concord of sweet sounds, / Is fit for treasons, stratagems and spoils."

—William Shakespeare, *The Merchant of Venice*, 1596–97

20 __ __

20 __ __

20 __ __

20 __ __

20 __ __

SEPTEMBER 5

"It is true of the Nation, as of the individual that the greatest doer must also be a great dreamer."

—Theodore Roosevelt, speech, 1905

20 __ __

20 __ __

20 __ __

20 __ __

20 __ __

SEPTEMBER 6

"From hence, ye beauties, undeceived, / Know, one false step is ne'er retrieved, / And be with caution bold."

—Thomas Gray, "Ode on the Death of a Favourite Cat, Drowned in a Tub of Goldfishes," 1748

20 __ __

20 __ __

20 __ __

20 __ __

20 __ __

SEPTEMBER 7

"In infinite time, in infinite matter, in infinite space, is formed a bubble organism, and that bubble lasts a while and bursts, and that bubble is Me."

—Leo Tolstoy, *Anna Karenina*, 1877

20 __ __

20 __ __

20 __ __

20 __ __

20 __ __

SEPTEMBER 8

"Old wood best to burn, old wine to drink, old friends to trust, and old authors to read."

—Francis Bacon, *Apothegms*, 1625

20 __ __

20 __ __

20 __ __

20 __ __

20 __ __

SEPTEMBER 9

"For art may err, but Nature cannot miss."

—John Dryden, *Fables Ancient and Modern*, 1700

20 __ __

20 __ __

20 __ __

20 __ __

20 __ __

SEPTEMBER 10

"The partisan, when he is engaged in a dispute, cares nothing about the rights of the question, but is anxious only to convince his hearers of his own assertions."

—Plato, *Phaedo*, fourth century BCE

20 __ __

20 __ __

20 __ __

20 __ __

20 __ __

SEPTEMBER 11

"When to the sessions of sweet silent thought
I summon up remembrance of things past."

—William Shakespeare, "Sonnet 30," 1609

20 __ __

20 __ __

20 __ __

20 __ __

20 __ __

SEPTEMBER 12

"Autumn, decking decay with such bright beauty, shedding a parting halo on the fading year; concentrating all of loveliness in that sweet, dreamy pensiveness."

—Grace Aguilar, *Home Scenes and Heart Studies*, 1878

20 __ __

20 __ __

20 __ __

20 __ __

20 __ __

SEPTEMBER 13

"You're obstinate, pliant, merry, morose, all at once. For me, there's no living with you, or without you."

—Martial, *Epigrams*, first century CE

20__ __

20__ __

20__ __

20__ __

20__ __

SEPTEMBER 14

"Little said is soon amended."

—Miguel de Cervantes, *Don Quixote*, 1612

20 __ __

20 __ __

20 __ __

20 __ __

20 __ __

SEPTEMBER 15

"How shall the ritual, then, be read?—the requiem how be sung
By you—by yours, the evil eye,—by yours, the slanderous tongue
That did to death the innocent that died, and died so young?"

—Edgar Allan Poe, "Lenore," 1843

20 __ __

20 __ __

20 __ __

20 __ __

20 __ __

SEPTEMBER 16

"Better the day, better the deed."

—Thomas Middleton, *Michaelmas Term*, 1604

20 __ __

20 __ __

20 __ __

20 __ __

20 __ __

SEPTEMBER 17

"There are three faithful friends—an old wife, an old dog, and ready money."

—Benjamin Franklin, *Poor Richard's Almanack*, 1758

20 __ __

20 __ __

20 __ __

20 __ __

20 __ __

SEPTEMBER 18

"There was nothing to do but to dig away at the base of this mountain of ignorance and prejudice."

—Upton Sinclair, *The Jungle*, 1905–06

20 __ __

20 __ __

20 __ __

20 __ __

20 __ __

SEPTEMBER 19

"How much a dunce, that has been sent to roam,
excels a dunce that has been kept at home."

—William Cowper, "The Progress of Error," 1782

20 __ __

20 __ __

20 __ __

20 __ __

20 __ __

SEPTEMBER 20

"Say not you know another entirely, till you have divided an inheritance with him."

—Johann Kaspar Lavater, *Aphorisms on Man*, 1788

20 __ __

20 __ __

20 __ __

20 __ __

20 __ __

SEPTEMBER 21

"And here poor fool! With all my lore I stand no wiser than before."

—Johann Wolfgang von Goethe, *Faust*, 1808

20 __ __

20 __ __

20 __ __

20 __ __

20 __ __

SEPTEMBER 22

"For what do we live, but to make sport for our neighbors, and laugh at them in our turn?"

—Jane Austen, *Pride and Prejudice*, 1813

20__ __

20__ __

20__ __

20__ __

20__ __

SEPTEMBER 23

"A sharp tongue is the only edged tool that grows keener with use."

—Washington Irving, *The Sketch Book*, 1819

20 __ __

20 __ __

20 __ __

20 __ __

20 __ __

SEPTEMBER 24

"Sadder than owl songs or the midnight blast
is that portentous phrase, 'I told you so.'"

—Lord Byron, *Don Juan*, 1819

20 __ __

20 __ __

20 __ __

20 __ __

20 __ __

SEPTEMBER 25

"Beauty without grace is the hook without the bait."

—Ralph Waldo Emerson, *The Conduct of Life*, 1860

20 __ __

20 __ __

20 __ __

20 __ __

20 __ __

SEPTEMBER 26

"If man were wholly ignorant of himself he would have no poetry in him, for one cannot describe what one does not conceive."

—Alexis de Tocqueville, *Democracy in America*, 1835

20 __ __

20 __ __

20 __ __

20 __ __

20 __ __

SEPTEMBER 27

"The public appears disposed to be amused even when they are conscious of being deceived."

—P. T. Barnum, *The Life of P. T. Barnum*, 1855

20 __ __

20 __ __

20 __ __

20 __ __

20 __ __

SEPTEMBER 28

"Subdue your appetites, my dears, and you've conquered human nature."

—Charles Dickens, *Nicholas Nickleby*, 1838

20 __ __

20 __ __

20 __ __

20 __ __

20 __ __

SEPTEMBER 29

"'You shall have my chairs and candle, / And my jug without a handle! / Gaze upon the rolling deep / (Fish is plentiful and cheap); / As the sea, my love is deep!'"

—Edward Lear, "The Courtship of the Yonghy-Bonghy-Bo," 1894

20 __ __ ______________________________

____

____

20 __ __ ______________________________

____

____

20 __ __ ______________________________

____

____

20 __ __ ______________________________

____

____

20 __ __ ______________________________

____

____

SEPTEMBER 30

"If I knew for a certainty that a man was coming to my house with the conscious design of doing me good, I should run for my life."

—Henry David Thoreau, *Walden*, 1854

20 __ __

20 __ __

20 __ __

20 __ __

20 __ __

OCTOBER 1

"You start a question, and it's like starting a stone. You sit quietly on the top of a hill; and away the stone goes, starting others."

—Robert Louis Stevenson, *Dr. Jekyll and Mr. Hyde*, 1886

20 __ __

20 __ __

20 __ __

20 __ __

20 __ __

OCTOBER 2

"This life is a hospital, where each patient is possessed by a desire to change beds."

—Charles Baudelaire, *Le Spleen de Paris*, 1869

20 __ __

20 __ __

20 __ __

20 __ __

20 __ __

OCTOBER 3

"I was benevolent and good; misery made me a fiend. Make me happy, and I shall again be virtuous."

—Mary Wollstonecraft Shelley, *Frankenstein*, 1818

20 __ __

20 __ __

20 __ __

20 __ __

20 __ __

OCTOBER 4

"Life is the art of drawing sufficient conclusions from insufficient premises."

—Samuel Butler, *The Way of All Flesh*, 1903

20 __ __

20 __ __

20 __ __

20 __ __

20 __ __

OCTOBER 5

"I thought in my heart how seldom, even in this world, justice fails to overtake the murderer, and to enforce the righteous judgment of God, 'that whoso sheddeth man's blood, by man shall his blood be shed.'"

—John William Polidori, *The Vampyre*, 1819

20 __ __

20 __ __

20 __ __

20 __ __

20 __ __

OCTOBER 6

"Life starts all over again when it gets crisp in fall."

—F. Scott Fitzgerald, *The Great Gatsby*, 1925

20 __ __

20 __ __

20 __ __

20 __ __

20 __ __

OCTOBER 7

"A great nose indicates a great man.
Genial, courteous, intellectual, virile, courageous."

—Edmond Rostand, *Cyrano de Bergerac*, 1897

20 __ __

20 __ __

20 __ __

20 __ __

20 __ __

OCTOBER 8

"I'm living so far beyond my income that we may almost be said to be living apart."

—Saki, *The Unbearable Bassington*, 1912

20 __ __

20 __ __

20 __ __

20 __ __

20 __ __

OCTOBER 9

"Every public action, which is not customary, either is wrong, or, if it is right, is a dangerous precedent. It follows that nothing should ever be done for the first time."

—F. M. Cornford, *Microcosmographia Academica*, 1908

20 __ __

20 __ __

20 __ __

20 __ __

20 __ __

OCTOBER 10

"From even the greatest of horrors irony is seldom absent."

—H. P. Lovecraft, *The Shunned House*, 1924

20 __ __

20 __ __

20 __ __

20 __ __

20 __ __

OCTOBER 11

"Life is a foreign language; all men mispronounce it."

—Christopher Morley, *Thunder on the Left*, 1925

20 __ __

20 __ __

20 __ __

20 __ __

20 __ __

OCTOBER 12

"Four be the things I am wiser to know:
Idleness, sorrow, a friend, and a foe."

—Dorothy Parker, "Inventory," 1926

20 __ __

20 __ __

20 __ __

20 __ __

20 __ __

OCTOBER 13

"It is the pup's mother teaches it to fight, and women know that fighting is a necessary art although men pretend there are others that are better."

—James Stephens, *The Boyhood of Fionn*, 1920

20 __ __

20 __ __

20 __ __

20 __ __

20 __ __

OCTOBER 14

"She had not known the weight until she felt the freedom."

—Nathaniel Hawthorne, *The Scarlet Letter*, 1850

20 __ __

20 __ __

20 __ __

20 __ __

20 __ __

OCTOBER 15

"What we have loved, / Others will love, and we will teach them how."

—William Wordsworth, *The Prelude*, 1850

20__ __

20__ __

20__ __

20__ __

20__ __

OCTOBER 16

"Such sweet compulsion doth in music lie."

—John Milton, *Arcades*, 1634

20 __ __

20 __ __

20 __ __

20 __ __

20 __ __

OCTOBER 17

"I am not imposed upon by fine words; I can see what actions mean."

—George Eliot, *The Mill on the Floss*, 1860

20 __ __

20 __ __

20 __ __

20 __ __

20 __ __

OCTOBER 18

"Art is a human activity having for its purpose the transmission to others of the highest and the best feelings to which men have risen."

—Leo Tolstoy, *What Is Art?*, 1897

20__ __

20__ __

20__ __

20__ __

20__ __

OCTOBER 19

"Taking a new step, uttering a new word, is what people fear most."

—Fyodor Dostoyevsky, *Crime and Punishment*, 1866

20 __ __

20 __ __

20 __ __

20 __ __

20 __ __

OCTOBER 20

"We all travel the Milky Way together, trees and men."

—John Muir, *The Mountains of California*, 1894

20 __ __

20 __ __

20 __ __

20 __ __

20 __ __

OCTOBER 21

"Seven years would be insufficient to make some people acquainted with each other, and seven days are more than enough for others."

—Jane Austen, *Sense and Sensibility*, 1811

20__ __

20__ __

20__ __

20__ __

20__ __

OCTOBER 22

"We are asleep until we fall in love."

—Leo Tolstoy, *War and Peace*, 1865

20__ __

20__ __

20__ __

20__ __

20__ __

OCTOBER 23

"Give sorrow words; the grief that does not speak
Whispers the o'er-fraught heart and bids it break."

—William Shakespeare, *Macbeth*, 1606

20 __ __

20 __ __

20 __ __

20 __ __

20 __ __

OCTOBER 24

"And now have I not told you that what you mistake for madness is but over acuteness of the senses?"

—Edgar Allan Poe, "The Tell-Tale Heart," 1843

20 __ __

20 __ __

20 __ __

20 __ __

20 __ __

OCTOBER 25

"But dreams come through stone walls, light up dark rooms, or darken light ones, and their persons make their exits and their entrances as they please, and laugh at locksmiths."

—Sheridan Le Fanu, *Carmilla*, 1872

20 __ __

20 __ __

20 __ __

20 __ __

20 __ __

OCTOBER 26

"Days decrease, / And autumn grows, autumn in everything."

—Robert Browning, "Andrea del Sarto," 1855

20 __ __

20 __ __

20 __ __

20 __ __

20 __ __

OCTOBER 27

"For to accuse requires less eloquence, such is man's nature, than to excuse; and condemnation, than absolution, more resembles justice."

—Thomas Hobbes, *Leviathan*, 1651

20 __ __

20 __ __

20 __ __

20 __ __

20 __ __

OCTOBER 28

"Treachery and violence are spears pointed at both ends; they wound those who resort to them worse than their enemies."

—Emily Brontë, *Wuthering Heights*, 1847

20 __ __

20 __ __

20 __ __

20 __ __

20 __ __

OCTOBER 29

"Ambrosio was yet to learn, that to a heart unacquainted with her, Vice is ever most dangerous when lurking behind the Mask of Virtue."

—Matthew Gregory Lewis, *The Monk*, 1796

20 __ __

20 __ __

20 __ __

20 __ __

20 __ __

OCTOBER 30

"Remember, too, that one act of beneficence, one act of real usefulness, is worth all the abstract sentiment in the world. Sentiment is a disgrace, instead of an ornament, unless it lead us to good actions."

—Ann Radcliffe, *The Mysteries of Udolpho*, 1794

20 __ __

20 __ __

20 __ __

20 __ __

20 __ __

OCTOBER 31

"Listen to them—the children of the night. What music they make!"

—Bram Stoker, *Dracula*, 1897

20 __ __

20 __ __

20 __ __

20 __ __

20 __ __

NOVEMBER 1

"Whenever I find myself growing grim about the mouth; whenever it is a damp, drizzly November in my soul . . ."

—Herman Melville, *Moby Dick*, 1851

20 __ __

20 __ __

20 __ __

20 __ __

20 __ __

NOVEMBER 2

"The Frost performs its secret ministry,
Unhelped by any wind."

—Samuel Taylor Coleridge, "Frost at Midnight," 1798

20 __ __

20 __ __

20 __ __

20 __ __

20 __ __

NOVEMBER 3

"That I could think there trembled through / His happy good-night air / Some blessed Hope, whereof he knew / And I was unaware."

—Thomas Hardy, "The Darkling Thrush," 1900

20 __ __

20 __ __

20 __ __

20 __ __

20 __ __

NOVEMBER 4

"For revenge is always the delight of a mean spirit, of a weak and petty mind!"

—Juvenal, "Satire XIII," ca. second century CE

20 __ __

20 __ __

20 __ __

20 __ __

20 __ __

NOVEMBER 5

"'Over the Mountains / Of the Moon, / Down the Valley of the Shadow, / Ride, boldly ride,' / The shade replied,— / 'If you seek for Eldorado!'"

—Edgar Allan Poe, "Eldorado," 1849

20 __ __

20 __ __

20 __ __

20 __ __

20 __ __

NOVEMBER 6

"'Build me straight, O worthy Master! / Stanch and strong, a goodly vessel.'"

—Henry Wadsworth Longfellow, "The Building of the Ship," 1849

20 __ __

20 __ __

20 __ __

20 __ __

20 __ __

NOVEMBER 7

"Herein lies the tragedy of the age: not that men are poor, — all men know something of poverty; not that men are wicked, — who is good? Not that men are ignorant, — what is Truth? Nay, but that men know so little of men."

—W.E.B. Du Bois, *The Souls of Black Folk*, 1903

20 __ __

20 __ __

20 __ __

20 __ __

20 __ __

NOVEMBER 8

"Life is not a matter of holding good cards,
but sometimes playing a poor hand well."

—Jack London, "To Build a Fire," 1908

20 __ __

20 __ __

20 __ __

20 __ __

20 __ __

NOVEMBER 9

"Further, nothing, except sin, is contrary to an act of virtue. But war is contrary to peace. Therefore war is always a sin."

—Saint Thomas Aquinas, *Summa Theologica*, ca. late thirteenth century

20 __ __

20 __ __

20 __ __

20 __ __

20 __ __

NOVEMBER 10

"The lion cannot protect himself from traps,
and the fox cannot defend himself from wolves. One must therefore
be a fox to recognize traps, and a lion to frighten wolves."

—Niccolò Machiavelli, *The Prince*, 1532

20 __ __

20 __ __

20 __ __

20 __ __

20 __ __

NOVEMBER 11

"If you trap the moment before it is ripe,
The tears of repentance you'll certainly wipe."

—William Blake, "Gnomic Verses," ca. 1783–1818

20 __ __

20 __ __

20 __ __

20 __ __

20 __ __

NOVEMBER 12

"Like the dew on the mountain, / Like the foam on the river, / Like the bubble on the fountain, / Thou art gone, and forever!"

—Sir Walter Scott, "The Lady of the Lake," 1810

20 __ __

20 __ __

20 __ __

20 __ __

20 __ __

NOVEMBER 13

"Nowadays people know the price of everything and the value of nothing."

—Oscar Wilde, *The Picture of Dorian Gray*, 1890

20 __ __

20 __ __

20 __ __

20 __ __

20 __ __

NOVEMBER 14

"I do not wish any reward but to know I have done the right thing."

—Mark Twain, *Adventures of Huckleberry Finn*, 1884

20 __ __

20 __ __

20 __ __

20 __ __

20 __ __

NOVEMBER 15

"November chill blaws loud wi' angry sugh; / The short'ning winter-day is near a close; / The miry beasts retreating frae the pleugh; / The black'ning trains o' craws to their repose."

—Robert Burns, "The Cotter's Saturday Night," 1786

20 __ __

20 __ __

20 __ __

20 __ __

20 __ __

NOVEMBER 16

"Batter my heart, three person'd God; for you / As yet but knock, breathe, shine and seek to mend."

—John Donne, *Holy Sonnets*, 1633

20 __ __

20 __ __

20 __ __

20 __ __

20 __ __

NOVEMBER 17

"Ye monsters of the bubbling deep, / Your Maker's praises spout; / Up from the sands ye codlings peep, / And wag your tails about."

—Cotton Mather, *The Wonders of the Invisible World*, 1693

20 __ __

20 __ __

20 __ __

20 __ __

20 __ __

NOVEMBER 18

"Better is bread with a happy heart, than wealth with vexation."

—Amenemope, *The Instruction of Amenemope*, ca. 1300 BCE

20 __ __

20 __ __

20 __ __

20 __ __

20 __ __

NOVEMBER 19

"My morning incense, and my evening meal,
The sweets of Hasty Pudding."

—Joel Barlow, "The Hasty Pudding," 1793

20 __ __

20 __ __

20 __ __

20 __ __

20 __ __

NOVEMBER 20

"They shall know, at least, that we possessed affections, which, running backward and warming with gratitude for what our ancestors have done for our happiness, run forward also to our posterity."

—Daniel Webster, "Plymouth Oration," 1820

20 __ __

20 __ __

20 __ __

20 __ __

20 __ __

NOVEMBER 21

"Come, ye thankful people, come,
Raise the song of harvest home."

—Henry Alford, "Come, Ye Thankful People, Come," 1844

20 __ __

20 __ __

20 __ __

20 __ __

20 __ __

NOVEMBER 22

"From the east to the west blow the trumpet to arms!
Through the land let the sound of it flee."

—Thomas Paine, "Liberty Tree," 1775

20 __ __

20 __ __

20 __ __

20 __ __

20 __ __

NOVEMBER 23

"Every trail has its end, and every calamity brings its lesson!"

—James Fenimore Cooper, *The Last of the Mohicans*, 1826

20 __ __

20 __ __

20 __ __

20 __ __

20 __ __

NOVEMBER 24

"The difference between treason and patriotism is only a matter of dates."

—Alexandre Dumas, *The Count of Monte Cristo*, 1844

20 __ __

20 __ __

20 __ __

20 __ __

20 __ __

NOVEMBER 25

"There was no use in trying to emancipate a wife
who had not the dimmest notion that she was not free."

—Edith Wharton, *The Age of Innocence*, 1920

20 __ __

20 __ __

20 __ __

20 __ __

20 __ __

NOVEMBER 26

"Step softly, under snow or rain, / To find the place where men can pray, / The way is all so very plain, / That we may lose the way."

—G. K. Chesterton, "The Wise Men," 1912

20 __ __

20 __ __

20 __ __

20 __ __

20 __ __

NOVEMBER 27

"Wisdom comes through suffering. / Trouble, with its memories of pain, / Drips in our hearts as we try to sleep, / So men against their will / Learn to practice moderation."

—Aeschylus, *The Oresteia*, 485 BCE

20 __ __

20 __ __

20 __ __

20 __ __

20 __ __

NOVEMBER 28

"How like winter has my absence been."

—William Shakespeare, "Sonnet 97," 1609

20 __ __

20 __ __

20 __ __

20 __ __

20 __ __

NOVEMBER 29

"Oh, thou art fairer than the evening air,
Clad in the beauty of a thousand stars."

—Christopher Marlowe, *The Tragical History of Doctor Faustus*, 1592

20 __ __

20 __ __

20 __ __

20 __ __

20 __ __

NOVEMBER 30

"The green mountain always lifts up its legs;
you don't need to carry a lantern in the daylight."

—Wanshi Shogaku, Buddhist koan, ca. 1200 CE

20 __ __

20 __ __

20 __ __

20 __ __

20 __ __

DECEMBER 1

"What a terrible blow would fall upon all professions if a teacher should be forbidden to speak upon things of which he knew nothing, and to an audience who knew more about them than he!"

—Henry Ward Beecher, "Political Economy of the Apple," 1859

20 __ __

20 __ __

20 __ __

20 __ __

20 __ __

DECEMBER 2

"Pleasure is a vain illusion; she draws you on to a thousand follies, errors, and I may say vices, and then leaves you to deplore your thoughtless credulity."

—Susanna Rowson, *Charlotte Temple*, 1791

20 __ __

20 __ __

20 __ __

20 __ __

20 __ __

DECEMBER 3

"Smiles and tears are so alike with me, they are neither of them confined to any particular feelings: I often cry when I am happy, and smile when I am sad."

—Anne Brontë, *The Tenant of Wildfell Hall*, 1848

20 __ __

20 __ __

20 __ __

20 __ __

20 __ __

DECEMBER 4

"Education means emancipation. It means light and liberty."

—Frederick Douglass, speech, "Blessings of Liberty and Education," 1894

20 __ __

20 __ __

20 __ __

20 __ __

20 __ __

DECEMBER 5

"He cannot wisely consent to spend the best years of his life in getting ready to live."

—Horace Greeley, *What I Know of Farming*, 1871

20 __ __

20 __ __

20 __ __

20 __ __

20 __ __

DECEMBER 6

"The question is not, 'Can they reason?'
nor, 'Can they talk?' but 'Can they suffer?'"

—Jeremy Bentham, *The Principles of Morals and Legislation*, 1789

20 __ __

20 __ __

20 __ __

20 __ __

20 __ __

DECEMBER 7

"With joy and wonder fill the hero's thought. / Unknown the names, he yet admires the grace, / And bears aloft the fame and fortune of his race."

—Virgil, *Aeneid*, 29 BCE

20 __ __

20 __ __

20 __ __

20 __ __

20 __ __

DECEMBER 8

"Woman is born free and lives equal to man in her rights. Social distinctions can be based only on the common utility."

—Olympe de Gouges, *A Declaration of the Rights of Woman and the Female Citizen*, 1791

20__ __

20__ __

20__ __

20__ __

20__ __

DECEMBER 9

"I wonder if the snow loves the trees and fields, that it kisses them so gently? And then it covers them up snug, you know, with a white quilt; and perhaps it says, 'Go to sleep, darlings, till the summer comes again.'"

—Lewis Carroll, *Alice's Adventures in Wonderland*, 1865

20 __ __

20 __ __

20 __ __

20 __ __

20 __ __

DECEMBER 10

"Education never ends, Watson. It is a series of lessons, with the greatest for the last."

—Sir Arthur Conan Doyle, "His Last Bow," 1917

20__ __

20__ __

20__ __

20__ __

20__ __

DECEMBER 11

"You gave too much rein to your imagination. Imagination is a good servant, and a bad master. The simplest explanation is always the most likely."

—Agatha Christie, *The Mysterious Affair at Styles*, 1920

20 __ __

20 __ __

20 __ __

20 __ __

20 __ __

DECEMBER 12

"I will devote myself sincerely and without reservation to the general demolition of my opinions."

—René Descartes, *Discourse on the Method*, 1637

20__ __

20__ __

20__ __

20__ __

20__ __

DECEMBER 13

"Every traveler has a home of his own, and he learns to appreciate it the more from his wandering."

—Charles Dickens, *A Christmas Carol*, 1843

20 __ __

20 __ __

20 __ __

20 __ __

20 __ __

DECEMBER 14

"To lose one parent, Mr. Worthing, may be regarded as a misfortune; to lose both looks like carelessness."

—Oscar Wilde, *The Importance of Being Earnest*, 1895

20 __ __

20 __ __

20 __ __

20 __ __

20 __ __

DECEMBER 15

"Strength is incomprehensible by weakness, and, therefore, the more terrible."

—Nathaniel Hawthorne, *The House of the Seven Gables*, 1851

20 __ __

20 __ __

20 __ __

20 __ __

20 __ __

DECEMBER 16

"And forthwith their shrill little voices uprose on the air, singing one of the old-time carols that their forefathers composed in fields that were fallow and held by frost."

—Kenneth Grahame, *The Wind in the Willows*, 1908

20 __ __

20 __ __

20 __ __

20 __ __

20 __ __

DECEMBER 17

"But why—but why, my friend? There is no why. People do stupid things just because they do stupid things."

—Guy de Maupassant, "The Model," 1883

20 __ __

20 __ __

20 __ __

20 __ __

20 __ __

DECEMBER 18

"Your tale, sir, would cure deafness."

—William Shakespeare, *The Tempest*, 1610

20 __ __

20 __ __

20 __ __

20 __ __

20 __ __

DECEMBER 19

"Life is bristling with thorns, and I know no other remedy than to cultivate one's garden."

—Voltaire, *Candide*, 1759

20 __ __

20 __ __

20 __ __

20 __ __

20 __ __

DECEMBER 20

"Of course I was under the spell, and the wonderful part is that, even at the time, I perfectly knew I was."

—Henry James, *The Turn of the Screw*, 1898

20 __ __

20 __ __

20 __ __

20 __ __

20 __ __

DECEMBER 21

"All partings foreshadow the great final one."

—Charles Dickens, *Bleak House*, 1852

20__ __

20__ __

20__ __

20__ __

20__ __

DECEMBER 22

"The pale, cold light of the winter sunset did not beautify—it was like the light of truth itself."

—Willa Cather, *My Ántonia*, 1918

20 __ __

20 __ __

20 __ __

20 __ __

20 __ __

DECEMBER 23

"Nature's creative power is far beyond man's instinct of destruction."

—Jules Verne, *Twenty Thousand Leagues Under the Sea*, 1872

20__ __

20__ __

20__ __

20__ __

20__ __

DECEMBER 24

"Fine old Christmas, with the snowy hair and ruddy face, had done his duty that year in the noblest fashion, and had set off his rich gifts of warmth and color with all the heightening contrast of frost and snow."

—George Eliot, *The Mill on the Floss*, 1860

20 __ __

20 __ __

20 __ __

20 __ __

20 __ __

DECEMBER 25

"The rooms were very still while the pages were softly turned, and the winter sunshine crept in to touch the bright heads and serious faces with a Christmas greeting."

—Louisa May Alcott, *Little Women*, 1868

20 __ __

20 __ __

20 __ __

20 __ __

20 __ __

DECEMBER 26

"Silence is of different kinds and breathes different meanings."

—Charlotte Brontë, *Villette*, 1853

20 __ __ ______________________________

____

____

20 __ __ ______________________________

____

____

20 __ __ ______________________________

____

____

20 __ __ ______________________________

____

____

20 __ __ ______________________________

____

____

DECEMBER 27

"No sensible man ever engages, unprepared,
in a fencing match of words with a woman."

—Wilkie Collins, *The Woman in White*, 1859

20 __ __

20 __ __

20 __ __

20 __ __

20 __ __

DECEMBER 28

"Even the darkest night will end, and the sun will rise."

—Victor Hugo, *Les Misérables*, 1862

20 __ __

20 __ __

20 __ __

20 __ __

20 __ __

DECEMBER 29

"I hate to hear you talk about all women as if they were fine ladies instead of rational creatures. None of us want to be in calm waters all our lives."

—Jane Austen, *Persuasion*, 1817

20 __ __

20 __ __

20 __ __

20 __ __

20 __ __

DECEMBER 30

"I was promised on a time to have reason for my rhyme;
From that time unto this season, I received nor rhyme nor reason."

—Attributed to Edmund Spenser, in a note to Queen Elizabeth requesting payment for his poem *The Faerie Queene*, ca. 1590

20 __ __

20 __ __

20 __ __

20 __ __

20 __ __

DECEMBER 31

"Ring out the old, ring in the new, / Ring, happy bells, across the snow: / The year is going, let him go; / Ring out the false, ring in the true."

—Alfred, Lord Tennyson, "Ring Out, Wild Bells," 1850

20 __ __

20 __ __

20 __ __

20 __ __

20 __ __

BOOKS TO READ WISH LIST

ok	Author	Date Started	Date Finished
		__/__/__	__/__/__
		__/__/__	__/__/__
		__/__/__	__/__/__
		__/__/__	__/__/__
		__/__/__	__/__/__
		__/__/__	__/__/__
		__/__/__	__/__/__
		__/__/__	__/__/__
		__/__/__	__/__/__
		__/__/__	__/__/__
		__/__/__	__/__/__
		__/__/__	__/__/__
		__/__/__	__/__/__
		__/__/__	__/__/__
		__/__/__	__/__/__
		__/__/__	__/__/__
		__/__/__	__/__/__
		__/__/__	__/__/__
		__/__/__	__/__/__

BOOKS TO READ WISH LIST

Book	Author	Date Started	Date Finished
		___/___/___	___/___/___
		___/___/___	___/___/___
		___/___/___	___/___/___
		___/___/___	___/___/___
		___/___/___	___/___/___
		___/___/___	___/___/___
		___/___/___	___/___/___
		___/___/___	___/___/___
		___/___/___	___/___/___
		___/___/___	___/___/___
		___/___/___	___/___/___
		___/___/___	___/___/___
		___/___/___	___/___/___
		___/___/___	___/___/___
		___/___/___	___/___/___
		___/___/___	___/___/___
		___/___/___	___/___/___
		___/___/___	___/___/___
		___/___/___	___/___/___